THE BRAZEN SERPENT

EILÉAN NÍ CHUILLEANÁIN

THE BRAZEN SERPENT

Wake Forest University Press

Published in

North America by

Wake Forest University Press

in 1995.

Published in Ireland and

in the United Kingdom by

The Gallery Press.

Wake Forest University Press

Post Office Box 7333,

Winston-Salem, NC 27109

Text designed by Peter Fallon

Cover designed by Richard Hendel

Set in Garamond

Printed by Thomson-Shore

LC Card Number 94-61973

ISBN (cloth) 0-916390-65-9

ISBN (paper) 0-916390-64-0

Contents

And the Lord sent fiery serpents among the people, and they bit the people; and much people of Israel died . . .

And the Lord said unto Moses, Make thee a fiery serpent, and set it upon a pole: and it shall come to pass, that every one that is bitten, when he looketh upon it, shall live.

And Moses made a serpent of brass, and put it upon a pole, and it came to pass, that if a serpent had bitten any man, when he beheld the serpent of brass, he lived.

— Numbers, XXI, 6-9

TWO POEMS
1994

Fireman's Lift

I was standing beside you looking up
Through the big tree of the cupola
Where the church splits wide open to admit
Celestial choirs, the fall-out of brightness.

The Virgin was spiralling to heaven,
Hauled up in stages. Past mist and shining,
Teams of angelic arms were heaving,
Supporting, crowding her, and we stepped

Back, as the painter longed to
While his arm swept in the large strokes.
We saw the work entire, and how the light

Melted and faded bodies so that
Loose feet and elbows and staring eyes
Floated in the wide stone petticoat
Clear and free as weeds.

This is what love sees, that angle:
The crick in the branch loaded with fruit,
A jaw defining itself, a shoulder yoked,

The back making itself a roof
The legs a bridge, the hands
A crane and a cradle.

Their heads bowed over to reflect on her
Fair face and hair so like their own
As she passed through their hands. We saw them
Lifting her, the pillars of their arms

(Her face a capital leaning into an arch)
As the muscles clung and shifted
For a final purchase together
Under her weight as she came to the edge of the cloud.

Parma 1963 — Dublin 1994

Hair

She gets that dark red hair from her grandfather.
The morning he saw it had begun to grow
He stood clutching the marble of his bald head,
The towel still in his hand. He remembered the night
They were all shouting indoors and he was the one
Left in the yard, his temple pressed against the downpipe,
Aware, as the church bell struck, of the white presence of mist.

POEMS
1989-1993

The Architectural Metaphor

The guide in the flashing cap explains
The lie of the land.
The buildings of the convent, founded

Here, a good mile on the safe side of the border
Before the border was changed,
Are still partly a cloister.

This was the laundry. A mountain shadow steals
Through the room, shifts by piles of folded linen.
A radio whispers behind the wall:

Since there is nothing that speaks as clearly
As music, no other voice that says
Hold me I'm going . . . so faintly,

Now light scatters, a door opens, laughter breaks in,
A young girl barefoot, a man pushing her
Backwards against the hatch —

It flies up suddenly —
There lies the foundress, pale
In her funeral sheets, her face turned west

Searching for the rose-window. It shows her
What she never saw from any angle but this:
Weeds nested in the churchyard, catching the late sun,

Herself at fourteen stumbling downhill
And landing, and crouching to watch
The sly limbering of the bantam hen

Foraging between gravestones —
                              Help is at hand
Though out of reach:
                    The world not dead after all.

                                        1989

The Real Thing

The Book of Exits, miraculously copied
Here in this convent by an angel's hand,
Stands open on a lectern, grooved
Like the breast of a martyred deacon.

The bishop has ordered the windows bricked up on this side
Facing the fields beyond the city.
Lit by the glow from the cloister yard at noon
On Palm Sunday, Sister Custos
Exposes her major relic, the longest
Known fragment of the Brazen Serpent.

True stories wind and hang like this
Shuddering loop wreathed on a lapis lazuli
Frame. She says, this is the real thing.
She veils it again and locks up.
On the shelves behind her the treasures are lined.
The episcopal seal repeats every coil,
Stamped on all closures of each reliquary
Where the labels read: *Bones
Of Different Saints. Unknown.*

Her history is a blank sheet,
Her vows a folded paper locked like a well.
The torn end of the serpent
Tilts the lace edge of the veil.
The real thing, the one free foot kicking
Under the white sheet of history.

La Corona

Since the mother took to her bed
She cannot guess how they live downstairs.
She manages her time.

The Feast of the Four Crowned Martyrs
Was also her wedding day.
The relics are sewn into the hem of her shift.

The day of the eclipse
Fell on the feast of St Rita.
A flower from the Holy Thorn, brought home by pilgrims,
Bleeds as dry as paper between
Chasms of favoured pages, riven hymns
That slice her leatherbound Manual.

Through the high window light forces its wedge
To blot out the calendar; the mountainside
Flooding, the water fanned in veins, backs
Against a dark cloud with a bright snake at its edge.

A daughter, hair dripping,
Lands in the doorway, framed
In the glow from the votive lamp.
She dumps down tea on a tray
And is gone with a splash
Muttering about paying the milkman.

The old one shuffles weathered paper
Deals herself a new hand:
Five cards with black borders
And the heroes', her cousins'
Grey hatchet faces.

The Tale of Me

The child's teeth click against the marble.
Her ear is crushed cold against the slab,
The dredged flour almost brushed by her hair.
She traces with her eye her mother's hand.

The hand squashes flour and eggs to hide the yeast
And again it folds and wraps away
The breathing, slackening, raw loaf
That tried to grow and was twisted and turned back —

Like the man in the next room
Wrapped as Adam in broad leaves,
Hiding under the folded mountains that fell on him
When he called them to come and cover him over.

He lies folded around
The pain salting his belly and gut,
Lies still groaning: I am not I,
My story is knotted and
Sour like the bread she made.

All for You

Once beyond the gate of the strange stableyard, we dismount.
The donkey walks on, straight in at a wide door
And sticks his head in a manger.

The great staircase of the hall slouches back,
Sprawling between warm wings. It is for you.
As the steps wind and warp
Among the vaults, their thick ribs part; the doors
Of guardroom, chapel, storeroom
Swing wide and the breath of ovens
Flows out, the rage of brushwood,
The roots torn out and butchered.

It is for you, the dry fragrance of tea-chests
The tins shining in ranks, the ten-pound jars
Rich with shrivelled fruit. Where better to lie down
And sleep, along the labelled shelves,
With the key still in your pocket?

The Glass Garden

The spider's blessing on my shoulder holds me back —
A sleek trailing thread catching the light
Breaks off like a hesitant voice, a breathing
Silence binding, tracing me.

I've been in the orchard where
Holding long crooked guns
Massed men in steel caps
Full to the lip with grave life
Stood staring in arrested profile.

And I've been inside the house beyond the trees
Cut and lying open in segments:
The morning shone straight in at the two doors
Brushing the scrubbed floor, showing up
A hairline slit in the lens of my right eye,
Transparent, a swimming impulse,
A thread searching upstream.

A Glass House

The joists have become transparent —
I can see what they do downstairs,
The dark blue bottle on the laundry shelf,
The label turned in to the corner.

Relaxed like the sea flower
Both eyes drugged and wide
In the clear salty pool
Open to the tides, I am sinking

Past open globes of eyes.
I can see where the sandy floor
Brushes away; a cloud floats
Puffed into the shape of myself.

Crates of racing pigeons wait
Rustling on a platform.
How far do I need to travel
To understand their talk?

The Water Journey

I sent the girl to the well.
She walked up the main road as far as Tell's Cross,
Turned left over the stile and up the hill path.
I stood at the door to watch her coming down,
Her eyes fixed on the level of the water
Cushioned in her palms, wavering
Like the circles of grain in wood.

She stepped neatly down on the road;
The lads on bicycles cheered as they passed her
And her fingers shook and nearly leaked and lost it.
She took her time for the last fifty yards
Bringing it to the threshold and there I drank.

I said to the other sisters, each of you
Will have to do the same when your day comes.
This one has finished her turn,
She can go home with her wages;
She would hardly make it as far
As the well at the world's end.

Passing Over in Silence

She never told what she saw in the wood;
There were no words for the stench,
The floated offal, the burnt patches.
She kept the secret of the woman lying
In darkness breathing hard,
A hooked foot holding her down.
She held her peace about the man who waited
Beside the lettered slab.

He sang:

I went into the alehouse and called for a drink,
The girl behind the bar could not speak for tears,
The drops of beer flowed down the sides of the glass;
She wept to think of the pierced head,
The tears our Saviour shed.

Saint Margaret of Cortona

Patroness of the Lock Hospital, Townsend Street, Dublin

She had become, the preacher hollows his voice,
A name not to be spoken, the answer
To the witty man's loose riddle, what's she
That's neither maiden, widow nor wife?

A pause opens its jaws
In the annual panegyric,
The word *whore* prowling silent
Up and down the long aisle.

Under the flourishing canopy
Where trios of angels mime the last trombone,
Behind the silver commas of the shrine,
In the mine of the altar her teeth listen and smile.

She is still here, she refuses
To be consumed. The weight of her bones
Burns down through the mountain.
Her death did not make her like this;

Her eyes were hollowed
By the bloody scene: the wounds
In the body of her child's father
Tumbled in a ditch. The door was locked,
The names flew and multiplied; she turned
Her back but the names clustered and hung
Out of her shoulderbones
Like children swinging from a father's arm,
Their tucked-up feet skimming over the ground.

Our Lady of Youghal

Flowing and veiling and peeled back, the tide
Washed the bulk of timber
Beached on the mud, so heavy
Twelve horses could not pull it.

A lay brother rose at dawn, and saw it moved,
The weight melted away,
To the shore below the water-gate.
He rolled it easily as far as the cloister.

At rest on the lip of weathered
Rough steps and the icy pavement,
It paused among the kneeling poor
The bark still crude and whole.

It takes the blind man's fingers
Blessing himself in the entry
To find the secret water treasured
In the tree's elbow; he washes his eyes and sees
A leaf cutting its way to the air
Inside a tower of leaves,
The virgin's almond shrine, its ivory lids parting
Behind lids of gold, bursting out of the wood.

No Loads/No Clothing/Allowed/In the Library

You must go naked into the library.
That pure white gown
They hand you entering weighs nothing at all.
You put it on, surrender
Everything but a few blank pages.
They lend you a pencil that writes and rubs clean.

The supervisor has long fair hair.
You sit underground,
She sees you on a screen, white against a window,
A marble court beyond. Her gaze sharpens,
A strand of her hair gets frozen, permanently
Trapped in the woollen band the man beside her weaves.

Just so twelve years ago I went to the church
With my hair hanging down,
I left my money and keys, I was driven
In a car not my own. There was trouble
When they led us aside to sign the papers —
They wouldn't write a line till they had their fees.

We could not move, our time settled in ice.
Sharp eyes watched in the crowd:
The beggar opened his bottle of *Marie Celeste*
And waved it around; my stepfather
Drew out a concealed cheque book; in the gallery
Over our heads the musicians sounded a retreat.

.

The Bee and the Rapeseed

The spine of the mountain stretches
And the big silent machines
In the blue shadow — the pulleys,
The cribwork, chutes, their tongues and grooves
And sliding gear intact since those days —
Loom and stretch, tilted in a quarry that's hemmed
By yellow fields of rape, shoving closer,
Crowding even the cool air in the shaft of the mine,

While rape honey floods the plain, folding,
Dripping over the sharpened ledges.
Almshouses, their lintels low for bent age,
Have beehives in their gardens; the bee soars
Over tall gables, flashings and ridge-tiles
Clenched against the sky. She rises early;
The planted avenues direct her flight.
Crests and shadows of the hills appear, crisp

As the split edge of the apple,
Pure as her mind —
                    She smells
The rapeseed sharply fenced in fields.
The traces of coulter and harrow
Push through the yellow sour blooms.

The native red-ass bee is there before her,
Persuaded away from the cliff and heather.

A Note

There is a note of the time
The nurse went out of the room,
The water was heard flowing —
She has not forgotten the sound.
It penetrated her mind
Like the deep dints under the sand
That show when the wind blows in March
Hollow like eyes in masks —
The marks the locals name
Where the five fingers sank.
In March she will go there again
And see them like eyes that move,
As suddenly aware
As when the dark presence
Of the wild boar crossed her path
One day on the mountain road.

Home Town

The bus is late getting in to my home town.
I walk up the hill by the barracks,
Cutting through alleyways that jump at me.
They come bursting out of the walls
Just a minute before I began to feel them
Getting ready to arch and push. Here is the house.

Nobody who knows me knows where I am now.
I have a pocketful of gravel to wake my aunt sleeping
Behind the third dark window counting left over the bakery.
Here I will not be asked to repeat the story.
Between her and me and the hour of my birth
A broad stony stream is sliding
That changes its course with the floods of every spring.

'Following her coffin in a dream . . .'

Following her coffin in a dream
In the country of bells, his heart
Waits for the signal to beat
As the cramped forearm feels for the scythe.

A herd of old men shrinks to a file
In thick coats climbing singly.
The flexed ankle turns at the top of the stile,
The foot spreads to match the weathered flagstone,

The dry throat remembers thirst
At the fasting hour, the dizzy stomach of prayer.
The hair above his collar itches,
He looks down at the cap in his fingers.

The air's profile parting waves of grass
Cuts a path to the voices behind the yews;
The skin on the back of his hands tells him the way to go
Like the tide returning threading the mazes of sand.

'In the year of the hurricane . . .'

In the year of the hurricane
The sea rose as high as the church,
The waves were hollow, like a crypt.

When they were gone, the sand blown aside,
The bounds of ancient farms
Stuck up, stone on bare stone.

The high-waterline scored in rock
Begins our lives again.

Below it lace of tidemarks
Washed like nets, with trimming
Of cork and foam, the trailing skirts

Lapping and overlapping,
Are shelved like the webbed shawls
Of the child wrapped and cradled,
Fostered after the storm.

Following

So she follows the trail of her father's coat through the fair
Shouldering past beasts packed solid as books,
And the dealing men nearly as slow to give way —
A block of a belly, a back like a mountain,
A shifting elbow like a plumber's bend —
When she catches a glimpse of a shirt-cuff, a handkerchief,
Then the hard brim of his hat, skimming along,

Until she is tracing light footsteps
Across the shivering bog by starlight,
The dead corpse risen from the wakehouse
Gliding before her in a white habit.
The ground is forested with gesturing trunks,
Hands of women dragging needles,
Half-choked heads in the water of cuttings,
Mouths that roar like the noise of the fair day.

She comes to where he is seated
With whiskey poured out in two glasses
In a library where the light is clean,
His clothes all finely laundered,
Ironed facings and linings.
The smooth foxed leaf has been hidden
In a forest of fine shufflings,
The square of white linen
That held three drops
Of her heart's blood is shelved
Between the gatherings
That go to make a book —
The crushed flowers among the pages crack
The spine open, push the bindings apart.

Woman Shoeing a Horse

This is the path to the stile
And this is where I would stand —
The place is all thick with weeds.

I could see the line of her back and the flash of her hair
As she came from the fields at a call,
And then ten minutes wasted, all quiet

But the horse in the open air clanking his feet
Until the fire was roaring and the work began,
And the clattering and dancing.

I could see by her shoulders how her breath shifted
In the burst of heat, and the wide gesture of her free arm
As she lifted the weight and clung

Around the hoof. The hammer notes were flying
All urgent with fire and speed, and precise
With a finicky catch at the end —

But the noise I could not hear was the shock of air
Crashing into her lungs, the depth
Of the gasp as she turned with a ready hand

As the heat from the fire drew up the chimney,
The flame pressing, brushing out the last thread,
Constantly revising itself upwards to a pure line.

I closed my eyes, not to see the rider as he left.
When I opened them again the sheep were inching forward,
A flock of starlings had darkened the sky.

Daniel Grose

The breach widens at every push,
The copingstone falls
To shatter the paved floor.
Then silence for three centuries
While a taste for ruins develops.

Now the military draughtsman
Is training his eye
On the upright of the tower,
Noting the doors that open on treetops;
He catches the light in the elder branches
Rooted in the parapet, captures
The way the pierced loop keeps exactly
The dimensions of the first wounding,
Holding in the same spasm the same long view
Of field and river, cottage and rock
All the way to the deconsecrated
Abbey of the Five Wounds.

Where is the human figure
He needs to show the scale
And all the time that's passed
And how different things are now?

No crowds engaged in rape or killing,
No marshalling of boy soldiers,
No cutting the hair of novices.
The old woman by the oak tree
Can be pressed into service
To occupy the foreground.
Her feet are warmed by drifting leaves.

He stands too far away
To hear what she is saying,
How she routinely measures

The verse called the midwife's curse
On all that catches her eye, naming
The scholar's index finger, the piper's hunch,
The squint, the rub, the itch of every trade.

Vierge Ouvrante

Overhead on the ladder
A craftsman can be heard ascending
Balancing the hammer and nails.

He tacks up the photographs:
How can he hold in his head all the leaves of that tree
Whose roots are everywhere, whose seed
Outnumbers the spawn of the ocean?

The woman in an anorak, snapped
Face down in a drain, her bare arse
Signalling to helicopters, hardly
Finds room beside the man boldly
Laid out on the stone slab
As naked as an elephant.

Mercifully in the last room
Cameras are not allowed.
You have to do your best with glass and shadows
And the light shining along the passages of your skull
To capture her, to remember

The opening virgin, her petticoats
Shelved like the poplars of an avenue
That slip aside until she uncovers the scars,
The marks of the ropes that chafed and held her
So she could not move or write but only commit
To the long band of memory that bound her like a silkworm's
thread
The tearing, the long falling, the splashing and staining she
saw.
And as she unwinds she begins to spin like a dancer against the
clock
And in one minute the room is full of the stuff, sticky,

White as a blue-bleached sheet in the sun —
Till there is nothing left of the darkness you need
For the *camera oscura*,
Only the shining of the blank chronicle of thread.

Man Watching a Woman

The sound of everything folding into sleep,
A sense of being nowhere at all,
Set him on his way (traffic far off, and wind
In tall trees) to a back gate, a dark yard.
A path goes past the bins, the kitchen door,
Switches to a gravel walk by the windows
Lit softly above the privet hedge.
He stops and watches. He needs to see this:

A woman working late in the refectory,
Sewing a curtain, the lines of her face
Dropping into fatigue, severity, age,
The hair falling out of its clasp at her poll.
The hands are raised to thread the needle,
The tongue moves behind her lips.
He cannot see the feet or shoes, they are trapped
In toils of cloth. He is comforted.

He can move on, while the night combs out
Long rushing sounds into quiet,
On to the scene, the wide cafés —
Trombone music over polished tables.
He will watch the faces behind the bar, tired girls,
Their muscles bracing under breakers of music
And the weight of their balancing trays, drinks, ice
    and change.

The Pastoral Life

You remember how often we stopped
At that corner house to drink lemonade in the kitchen
And cycled on down to the harbour
The breeze filling our skirts.

But years later I passed their door,
Suddenly taking the mountain road.
I laboured up between rocks
Until when I turned east to the plain I heard

The corncrake in the shining grass.
The horses froze in troops of seven or eight
And a dull sound carried all that distance,
The bells around the necks of the leaders.

Will I ever go back? After the years I spent there
Depending on idleness that never let me down —
I waited for the wind to blow hairs in at my door
Carrying the story of the breed, for the right light
To show up the printing of muscle under the hide?
Could I go back after vesting my years

And leaving just once in November until the spring
When I found the plain blackened by fire
And staggered over bones too heavy for me to bury,

— Like finding a friend's ashes evenly shed
On the open page of a book?
                        I hear now, and believe it,
The grass has grown back,
                        the horses are breeding there again.

The Party Wall

We were all still living at home then,
In the house with the fancy grilles
And the tall iron gates that let us out
Gliding to business and back at night for our tea.
We rose one morning to find the garden
Drifted and crisped with stiff white feathers.
They shone bluish against the red brick walls,
As they shifted and settled in the draught from the street.

We were not shocked at all until the next day
When the aerial photographs were published
Showing the house that backed against ours
But looked away across the Avenue   •
Visited the same, its roof and courtyards
Blessed with angeldown and cobalt shadows.

The tenants had my grandfather's name.
I went on my bicycle to see Father Deveney
In his room in the old priests' home.
We sat at the window looking towards Mount Desert
And he ate sweets and told me he remembered
When that house too had been part of his parish.
But he had never been told my aunt's story
About all the trouble over building the party wall.

That Summer

So what did she do that summer
When they were all out working?

If she moved she felt a soft rattle
That settled like a purseful of small change.
She staggered through the quiet of the house,
Leaned on a flowering doorpost
And went back inside from the glare
Feeling in her skirt pocket the skin on her hands,
Never so smooth since her fourteenth year.

One warm evening they were late;
She walked across the yard with a can,
Watered a geranium and kept on going
Till she came to the ridge looking over the valley
At the low stacked hills, the steep ground
Between that plunged like a funnel of sand.
She couldn't face back home, they came for her
As she stood watching the hills breathing out and in,
Their dialogue of hither and yon.

The Secret

Instead of burning the book or getting its value
They hid it and were silent, even at home,
So that the history of that lost year
Remained for each one her own delusion.
As the memory faded they had to live.
No one would buy their blood, but they sold
Their hair, the milk from their breasts,
Their signatures on slips of ravelled paper,
The grazing as far as the drawing-room windows
And at last the fresh fine grass
That had started to grow under the first arch
Of the bridge beside the burnt-out paper-mill.

A Witness

Can I be the only one alive
Able to remember those times?
What keeps them from asking the others?

As I start on my dinner of dogfish and cockles
A draught blows the hinges and one of them shuffles
In on the floor to sound me about our troubles.

Though he's nearly as old as myself the grey hags in the corner
Are beginning to watch his motions
As he loses his pencil and the page in his notebook.

I tell him about the day the mouse tumbled
In the one jar of oil and my mother shouting
At the Yank captain that all her geese were stolen.

I fix my eye on the mountain across the valley
Where we all came from and on the one cloud stalling
Clamped on the wild shelf, that will not move away.

Beyond the walls I can hear the children playing
In the riverbed. If I could tell what they are crying
It would lighten my darkness like knowing the language
  of birds.

On the Day

Why is the room opened,
The man half-seen in shirtsleeves
With a click of forks being counted —

The glasses are lined on trays;
I cannot speak the reason
I am combing out the children's hair
Dragging teeth down through silence:

Because there is no time,
The fanned hand of cards is banged shut,
The melodeon's slow air tumbled and shrugged
Is boxed up small in an instant and kicked
Out of sight, under the bench in the kitchen.

A Posting

You are reaching me in translation,
A voice with no taste or weight,
In the tones of the hand-tinted early
Print of the Café du Port: palm trees,
Two men in white djellabas gravely smoking,
A light struggling to climb around
The bruised edges of a cloud,

A shadow burnt into the earth.
At the sound of the voice the sea is gone
The beach a rock-salty rainbow
The flat bay a sudden gulf, even crabs
Shuffled out of sight, even the word
Brushed out that would name the starshaped
Creature that clings to a rock shaped like a skull.

A Hand, A Wood

1

After three days I have to wash —
I am prising you from under my nails
Reluctantly, as time will deface
The tracks, their branching sequence,
The skill of the left and the right hand.

Your script curls on the labels of jars,
Naming pulses in the kitchen press.
The dates you marked in the diary come and pass.

2

The wet leaves are blowing, the sparse
Ashes are lodged under the trees in the wood
Where we cannot go in this weather.
The stream is full and rattling,
The hunters are scattering shot —
The birds fly up and spread out.

I am wearing your shape
Like a light shirt of flame;
My hair is full of shadows.

Studying the Language

On Sundays I watch the hermits coming out of their holes
Into the light. Their cliff is as full as a hive.
They crowd together on warm shoulders of rock
Where the sun has been shining, their joints crackle.
They begin to talk after a while.
I listen to their accents, they are not all
From this island, not all old,
Not even, I think, all masculine.

They are so wise, they do not pretend to see me.
They drink from the scattered pools of melted snow:
I walk right by them and drink when they have done.
I can see the marks of chains around their feet.

I call this my work, these decades and stations —
Because, without these, I would be a stranger here.